D1499057

little feet

Great "feats" begin with lil' steps!

Marina

Château de Blanville, *St-Luperce, France*

little feet

photographs by MARINA DRASNIN GILBOA

CHRONICLE BOOKS
SAN FRANCISCO

Copyright © 2000 Chronicle Books. All rights reserved. No part of this book may be reproduced
in any form without written permission from the publisher.

Library of Congress Cataloging-in-Publication Data:
Gilboa, Marina Drasnin.

      Little feet / photographs by Marina Drasnin Gilboa

      p.   cm.

      ISBN 0-8118-2452-7

      1. Photography, artistic. 2. Gilboa, Marina Drasnin. 3. Foot—European pictorial works.

      4. Shoes—European pictorial works. 5. Toddlers—pictorial works. I. Title.

TR654.G547 2000

779' . 25'092—dc21   99-33592

                      CIP

Printed in Singapore

Design: Henry Quiroga

Distributed in Canada by Raincoast Books
8680 Cambie Street
Vancouver, BC V6P 6M9

10 9 8 7 6 5 4 3 2 1

Chronicle Books
85 Second Street
San Francisco, CA 94105

www.chroniclebooks.com

I dedicate this book to my husband, Tsach Gilboa, my inspiration and life partner whose love, support, and encouragement took me on the greatest adventure of my life—an adventure that is still going strong!

Acknowledgments

It is with joy that I want to thank my wonderful family whose artistic talents and originality have inspired and influenced me since birth. Trisha, Suzy, Peter, and Alison . . . what a design team. To my amazing parents, Sidney and Virginia Drasnin, artists extraordinaire, there are no words to express my gratitude. I thank you from the bottom of my heart. Everything I am and strive to be in my life is by your example and encouragement.

There are so many friends who supported and cheered me on over the years. To name a few: Zia Barbara, Marina pìccola, Rhonda, Carol, Sara, Laurie, Taf, Tai, Rand, Neda, Maddie, Sunday, Diana, Karla, Aime, Gigi, Josie, Cami, Kathy, Rachel, Diane, my sweet Adele and angel Sarah.

And to Nion McEvoy and Christina Wilson at Chronicle Books for your wonderful enthusiasm.

And to my son, Harrison Gabriel Gilboa, for bringing joy and inspiration to my world. You will always be my greatest and most beautiful work of art.

Fisherman's Wharf, *San Francisco, California, U.S.A.*

When my wife told me about her idea for *Little Feet* I was intrigued. When she said, "We need the right shoes and the right environment—this project requires Europe," I was convinced. So off we went to France, Italy, and Great Britain.

Our son Harrison wasn't born yet, so I wasn't sure how parents would react to my wife chasing their children around the park to immortalize their feet. "Don't worry," she said, "people are nice and it is only their precious little feet I want anyway . . . It's not like I'm stealing their souls—or even their soles!" I tried not to worry.

We are walkers by nature and camera-carrying walkers by choice. You never know when you are going to run into that great shot, and the next great shot, and the next. . . . Over a period of several years Marina made a point of hanging out in the beautiful European parks, a favorite locale for "little feet." She always asked the parents first, and often sent them copies of the photographs, and sometimes made friends.

Although not all of the "little feet" we photographed are included here, they are all beautiful and as precious to their parents as our son's are to us. As you know, they don't stay "little feet" for long and when they grow they are somehow not quite as delicious.

—*Tsach Gilboa*

Via della Scrofa, *Rome, Italy*

Bar-sur-Loup, *France*

Saint-Quentin la Poterie, *France*

St-Paul de Vence, *France*

Stone Manor, *Malibu, California, U.S.A.*

Saint-Malo, *France*

Venice, *California, U.S.A.*

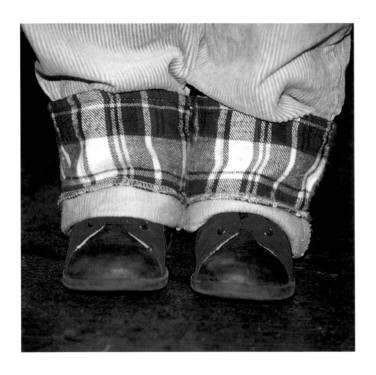

British Museum, *London, England*

Vancouver, *British Columbia, Canada*

Stratford-upon-Avon, *England*

Pont-Saint-Louis en l'Île, *Paris, France*

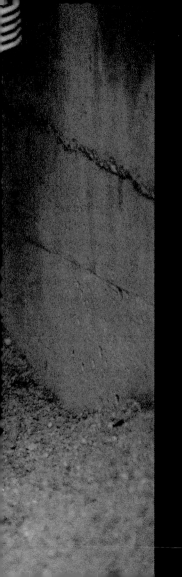

Brantôme, *France*

Palais Royal, *Paris, France*

Gourdon, *France*

La Chorane, *Tourrettes-sur-Loup, France*

Pacific Palisades, *California, U.S.A.*

Saint-Tropez, *France*

Santa Monica, *California, U.S.A.*

Fontainebleau, *France*

Santa Monica, *California, U.S.A.*

Honfleur, *France*

Cross River, *New York, U.S.A*

dsor, England

Los Angeles, *California, U.S.A.*

Jardin du Luxembourg, *Paris, France*

Beverly Hills, *California, U.S.A.*

Jardin des Tuileries, *Paris, France*

Rue de Grenelle, *Paris, France*

Farmers' Market, *Santa Monica, California, U.S.A.*

St-Rémy-de-Provence, *France*

Siena, *Italy*

Rome, *Italy*

Parc de Bagatelle, *Paris, France*

Hagia Sofia, *Istanbul, Turkey*

Santa Monica, *California, U.S.A.*

San Diego, *California, U.S.A.*

Jardin du Luxembourg, *Paris, France*

Borghese Gardens, *Rome, Italy*

Parc de Monceau, *Paris, France*

Mont-St-Michel, *France*

in du Luxembourg, *Paris, France*

Snowbird, *Utah, U.S.A*

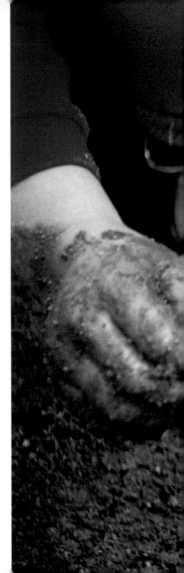

Santa Monica, *California, U.S.A.*

Jardin du Luxembourg, *Paris, France*

London, *England*

Santa Barbara, *California, U.S.A.*

Orcas Island, *Washington*

Borghese Gardens, *Rome, Italy*

Jardin du Luxembourg, *Paris, France*

Arles, *France*

Avignon, *France*

Tel Aviv, *Israel*

Jardin du Luxembourg, *Paris, France*